REFUSING THE VEIL

PROVOCATIONS

REFUSING THE VEIL

YASMIN ALIBHAI-BROWN

SERIES EDITOR:

YASMIN ALIBHAI-BROWN

Biteback Publishing

First published in Great Britain in 2014 by
Biteback Publishing Ltd
Westminster Tower
3 Albert Embankment
London SE1 7SP
Copyright © Yasmin Alibhai-Brown 2014

Yasmin Alibhai-Brown has asserted her right under the Copyright,
Designs and Patents Act 1988 to be identified as the author of this work.

ISBN 978-1-84954-750-5

10 9 8 7 6 5 4 3 2 1

A CIP catalogue record for this book is available from the British Library.

Set in Stempel Garamond

Printed and bound in Great Britain by
CPI Group (UK) Ltd, Croydon CR0 4YY

MIX
Paper from
responsible sources
FSC® C020471
www.fsc.org

Contents

Glossary

Common usage of these terms – I am listing the most common types.

ABAYA: Saudi long coat or cloak, mostly black.

BUIBUI: The same as a burkha, worn in Zanzibar and coastal areas of East Africa.

BURKHA: Full body and face covering, sometimes with lattice over the eyes.

CHADOR: Iranian, black, full-length, loose coat or cloak.

DEOBANDI: Established in 1867 in India, these Muslims follow a strict form of Sunni Islam based on certain texts and sources. A significant proportion of Muslim migrants to Europe follow these strictures.

EID: Two annual celebrations. One to mark the end of Ramadhan; the second honours Abraham who was ready to kill his son Isaac on the orders of God as a test of faith (this story is in the Book of Genesis).

FAKIR: In common usage, it is a person who gives up worldly goods and follows a life of mysticism and purity.

HAJJ: Annual pilgrimage to Mecca that is a duty for all Muslims. It honours Abraham who was ready to kill his son Isaac on the orders of God; it was a test of faith. This story is in the Book of Genesis. As men and women walk around the Kaaba (the block of stone covered in black), they pray as equals, humble before Allah. The experience brings elation, affirmation and renewal.

HIJAB: Head covering, including bands across foreheads and around the neck and shoulders.

ISLAMIC: Generic term used to describe faith or practice. So, for example, Islamic schools teach religion and behaviours expected of those who follow the faith.

ISLAMICIST: This term has come into usage since 9/11 and refers to those men or women who reject all other world faiths and various forms of worship in Islam. They also tend to promote political and social domination, sometimes violence.[1]

JILBAB: Full body coat or cloak.

MUFTI: A scholar and respected authority on Islam and Islamic law. Ayatollahs are the same. Imams tend to be more focussed on practice and are considered experts on what good Muslims should try to do. Some Muftis, Ayatollahs and Imams are flexible, wise and thoughtful; others are authoritarian.

NIQAB: Full body covering, including the face; only the eyes are visible.

---

1 An excellent book for this basic information is *Dictionary of Islam*, Azim Nanji, Penguin, 2008.

PACHELI: Light scarf, often coloured or patterned, made of silk or chiffon worn by some Shia Muslim women of Indian heritage. It is similar to scarves worn by Sikhs and some Hindus.

SALAFI: A nineteenth-century movement that is as rigid as Wahabism, though Salafis assert they are not the same. They emerged out of the fraught encounter between colonial Europeans and subjugated Arabs. In essence, they are literalists and purists who tolerate no dissent or choice in practice. The ideal is to return Islam to the days of the Prophet and replicate the lives of believers back then. Extremists tend to come from this intolerant doctrine.

SHALWAR KAMEEZ: Trousers and tunics worn across the Indian subcontinent and by British Asians of all faiths.

SHIA/SUNNI: After the death of the Prophet, early converts to Islam had to find a leader to guide them through the years that followed. They discussed, argued and disagreed over whom that should be and the basis of the selection. Succession divided Muslims and this schism, if anything, has become deeper and more violent in modern times. Some backed the claim of Ali ibn Abi Talib, Muhammad's son-in-law married to Fatima, which they

(Shias) believed was what the Prophet had decreed. Others, however, followed Abu Bakr, a trusted companion of the Prophet and father of young Aisha, who married Muhammad and led armies to fight Ali. These believers (Sunnis) are the dominant majority in Islam today.

SUFI: Muslims for whom Islam is a search for spirituality and an intense connection with God through meditation and personal struggle. They are guided by Imams as they go on a personal inner journey to salvation. It is the quietest and most introverted of Muslim faiths. Sufism is considered blasphemous by some hard-line Sunnis.

RAMADHAN: The month in the lunar calendar when Muslims fast all day, from sunrise to sunset. They do not eat or drink anything. It was one of the injunctions in an early revelation to the Prophet. The fast teaches discipline and empathy for the poor.

WAHABI: A form and doctrine of Islam, officially imposed in Saudi Arabia. An eighteenth-century Saudi cleric, Muhammad Abd al-Wahab (1703–92) started it all. He was puritanical and, with the support of some key tribal leaders including Ibn Saud, was able to establish a regional power base. His mission was uncompromising: it was to enforce his interpretation of Islam, which was rigid, regressive and punitive. All those who had 'strayed' from the only 'right' way were ungodly sinners who deserved no mercy. Shias, Sufis and other diverse Muslims were damned and attacked. Tombs of saints, and even historical sites connected to the life of the Prophet, were, and are still, being destroyed by Wahabis, for whom history ended after Allah selected his final messenger. Their influence now extends around the world.

A brief note

THIS TOPIC DIVIDES people. It will divide readers of this book too. Many of the women I truly respect, and some friends too, wear the hijab or jilbab. They are not made to do so, but feel that it keeps them within the fold, articulates their faith and gives them an identity in our increasingly homogenous world. For some, it is a way of placating their families so they can follow their dreams, go into higher education and the job market. Others consider the choice a political statement of power. I have met women in full niqab who are spirited and independent, so I am not suggesting this is simple oppression.

What I am saying, though, is that those women who take on these symbols do so without too many questions or without delving deep into the implications, back-stories and history. Their choice, even if independently made, is unexamined. Those countless Muslim females who are expected to do and wear as told don't ever ask why. This book is political, not personal. I want my hijabi friends, acquaintances and detractors to know I write it in good faith. I hope they read my arguments, even if to reject them roundly.

Part I

What I see;
what I hear;
what I fear

THERE ARE ONLY five fundamental obligations in Islam: faith in a merciful God whose messenger was Prophet Muhammad; fasting during Ramadhan; almsgiving; prayers; and pilgrimage to Mecca – only if the journey is affordable. None of those inhibit modern life, undermine human rights or equality. In fact the basic tenets of the religion affirm good, universal principles and teach humility. For example, those who have plenty, experience real hunger during Ramadhan, get to feel deprivation. Women and men are not separated during Hajj. When they die, Muslims – royals or paupers – are all wrapped in a plain white sheet and interred in simply marked graves. In the early days of Islam, women, including those in the Prophet's family, were conspicuous, active and powerful. His first wife – with whom he stayed till she died – was a businesswoman; his daughter Fatima commanded respect; and Aisha, his young wife, commanded armies.

So much has changed since then. Around the world, Islam has been distorted, corrupted and sullied by male theologians, chauvinist leaders and fake fakirs. I am a Muslim, flawed and sometimes full of doubt, but still a believer. Prayers give me solace, briefly taking me out of this world to intangible, numinous spaces.

I felt it was time, indeed my duty, to write a serious book on why I truly, deeply and keenly believe the veil, in all its permutations, is indefensible and unacceptable. Vast numbers of Muslim and other objectors daren't voice their views, but needs must. Muslim and non-Muslim champions of the veil say that this is a fuss about nothing important: it is simply another way the West picks on followers of Islam and, confusingly, that it is a requirement for true worshippers. They are being disingenuous or possibly naive. These pieces of cloth have become the flags of revolution and counter-revolution, of enforced conformity and sassiness, of tyranny and political resistance. Rows periodically burst out over the veil – bad dramas, full of commotion, which simply entrench positions.

One striking example demonstrates how contentious the issue has become. On 10 September 2013, Birmingham Metropolitan College issued new guidelines: on college premises, everyone was required to show their faces. Hoodies, caps and veils were not permitted. It was a perfectly reasonable directive. Nudists after all can't attend college stark naked. They have to compromise, follow regulations and recognise social conventions. Hood- and cap-wearers accepted the rule, but not veiled females. Thousands of students signed a petition; the college head, Dame Christine Braddock, was accused of 'Islamaphobia'. The rule was 'disgusting', they said, and an infringement of 'freedom'. Within three days the college surrendered and revoked the ordinance. The organised bullying and blackmailing was disgraceful, 'disgusting' even.

In 2014, a similar confrontation was provoked at the excellent Camden School for Girls. At the start of the academic year, a Muslim girl who had a place to study A levels turned up in full niqab. The school refused to let her into the class. An orchestrated bullying campaign was started to force the school to back down. As ever, some liberals came out against the school.[2]

Similar coordinated outrage is whipped up against politicians who raise objections to the niqab. In 2006, for example, Jack Straw was badly bruised by one such onslaught after he asked a constituent to remove her face cover. Straw has a mixed, at times dishonourable, record as an MP and minister, but on this he was right and within his rights. They shut him up fast. Some parliamentarians do harbour prejudices against Muslims. Not all of them do. A good number of them have genuine misgivings about veiling. And so they should. They must also be able to express their concerns in an open society.

---

2   See, for example, Gaby Hinsliff's column, 'The Niqab is No Reason to Deny a Girl an Education', *The Guardian*, 25 September 2014. The organisation Liberty also defends the right to veil on liberal grounds.

In the '70s, when I came to Britain, British Muslim females did not wear headscarves or body and face coverings. When oil-rich sheikhs turned up on shopping sprees with their veiled entourages, cartoonists enjoyed mocking them. Now veils are ubiquitous – a depressing and scary development. Do not believe those who say these clothes are adopted by only a small number of Muslims females. It is spreading across the country and in all classes. I live in west London, where entire localities now seem to be full of covered-up women – it started after the Saudis set up a school in Acton. At local Muslim celebrations, they keep out women who show their hair. I know, because it happened to me.

One saying attributed to the Prophet is this: 'God has not created anything better than reason, anything more perfect or beautiful than reason.'[3] Here, I use reason, argument, facts, personal experiences and history to back my viewpoint that Muslims, feminists and liberals of all shades should repudiate female body wraps.

---

3   This is a hadith – words of the Prophet recorded by scholars. See *The Book of Hadith*, Charles Guy Eaton, The Book Foundation, 2008.

Modern western life can be disorientating, meaning-less and amoral. It is materialistic, hedonistic, socially anarchic, sex-obsessed and atomised. Feminism is betrayed and humiliated by so-called 'girl power'. One sees young women in clothes that call out to men. Pre-teens, younger girls, sometimes toddlers, are dressed in flirty, foxy gear. The little ones are being trained to think of themselves primarily as eye candy and, in time, pullers and pleasers. Bovine followers of fash-ion are shaped by subliminal promotional messages; marketing and the media have successfully infiltrated their heads. These come-hither styles benefit only men and big businesses. Females become body parts, meat.

However, I believe strongly that cloaks, scarves and masks also degrade women by regarding them primar-ily as sexual creatures, but severely controlled ones. Again, the beneficiaries are men. They too are manip-ulated, though they would deny it. Half-naked lasses and young veiled women are an affront to female dig-nity, potential and autonomy. They are all marionettes in the hands of forces they do not understand and have internalised messages about femaleness. The only difference is that, with the exception of pimped sex workers, non-Muslim females are not forced into alluring clothes.

A moot question: Why is market-driven brainwashing scandalous, but brainwashing perpetrated through religious dogma perfectly respectable? Why are we allowed to question and criticise women in tarty clothes, but not hijabis?

*   *   *

IT WAS 22 July 2014. The sun had been shining for a fortnight. Zephyrs and occasional downpours cooled the air on some days, but not on this particular stifling Tuesday. At midday, I went to Ealing Common, which is right opposite my flat, and sat on a bench under a tree. No playful breeze lifted the leaves or wafted over the skin. It was officially one of the hottest days of the year.

A woman veiled in black, her hands gloved and feet in trainers, passed by slowly with a soft tread. I was wearing a midi-skirt, festooned with daisies, and a short-sleeved top – nothing immodest. She turned her face to me. It was covered, as so many are now all across Britain, but in her case, she had black gauze over her eyes too. Eyes must have become sluttish in the hardening rules of Wahabi Saudi Islam.

This woman's total negation of womanhood was mortifying. I couldn't smile at her because of all the tumultuous feelings she had generated in a fleeting encounter. I knew that if anyone had racially insulted her, I would instinctively have rushed to her defence, of course. But in my own head I hated what she was doing to herself and to the Sufi-type Islam with which I had grown up. The way we practised, and still practise, is open, lyrical, meditative, private, quiet, in the heart rather than noisily on the streets. Men and women are equal before God in mosque halls; women often lead prayers and hymns.

My reactions were probably unfair. What right did I have to be so censorious? Live and let live is the great British way. Only one can't. Not really. Clothes worn by women and men, girls and boys, are full of meanings and messages – intentional and unintentional. Advertising, psychology, physiology and social strictures

– societal changes determine buying and sartorial behaviours. A young boy from a housing estate who wears false designer sunglasses signals aspiration, self-consciousness, a need for respect, purchased élan. A baby dressed in real designer gear reflects snobbery, wealth, parental competition, purchased status. A young woman dressed like a lap dancer may be showing sexual confidence or a neediness to please. We all make judgements about appearances. Arguably, traditionalist Muslims are the most judgemental of all.

In 2013, when on a trip to India, I had tea with some desolate Indian Muslim men and women in Mumbai. They are a poor, discriminated-against, ill-educated and powerless minority in a nation increasingly dominated by aggressive Hindu nationalists. With all this to contend with, what did they want to talk about most? They wanted to know why European and American governments were making Muslims dress like streetwalkers and drink alcohol. They were convinced their co-religionists were hapless victims of state-ordered lifestyles.

Three years earlier, Sadakat Kadri, a British Muslim

barrister and author, had a similar conversation with orthodox Muslims in India when he told them that his mother and sister did not veil: 'A stressful silence ended only when someone suggested, with attempted kindness, that the British government had no business forcing women to lead such shameful lives.'[4]

Say the woman in the park actually wanted to mask her face and hide every inch of her skin. Well then, to me, she was acquiescing to and projecting religious misogyny and cultural disdain. Her slight glance was disconcerting and full of meanings I could only try to guess. Momentarily, I felt that by wearing summer clothes I was being cheap, offering myself up to male lasciviousness and dirty fantasies. Though that feeling didn't last, it was disconcerting.

But what if her unseen eyes were not reproaching but envying me? Was she made to wear the mournful shroud; to deny all the physical attributes that made her who she was, her unique humanity; to turn herself

---

4   The episode appears in his remarkable book, *Heaven on Earth: A Journey Through Shari'a Law*, Bodley Head, 2011, p. 174.

into a ghost before she had passed on? Was her niqab a sign of defiant pride or utter powerlessness?

I wanted to know what had led to her taking up the Taliban-approved kit; if she thought I was bad and she was good; whether I was bound to end up in hell and she had a guaranteed place in paradise. But we both knew there could be no conversation between us.

It was clear that only those of her tribe and gender could approach her. Her soft polyester was less penetrable than the thick walls and heavy doors of a prison or fortress. She was in a moving cell without a window or small opening – a space of absolute darkness. The sun, giver of life and joy, was firmly kept out. Her peripheral vision was more restricted than the view from a small letterbox. I smelt sweat and perfume on her – a sign that she wasn't indifferent to feminine artifice and allure. Maybe it was a subversive, olfactory message: I am still a woman, I am sensual and want attention. If it was her silent mutiny, it was pathetic. If it was a sign that she was just like any other fashionable woman, it was equally pathetic. I am sorry to sound so harsh – but those were my honest reactions.

I know these are the reactions of many others, although they don't openly express their revulsion for fear of encouraging racism (a very light sleeper that is always around and ready to pounce). I too am apprehensive that this book will give succour to the BNP, EDL and Britons who detest Muslims and other diverse populations. But in the end those people don't matter and can't matter. They hate us enough already.

No one really knows how many such women are coerced; how many feel this is what God wants; how many see veiling as a badge of honour; how many hope it will protect them; how many are being defiant in the face of real anti-Muslim prejudices. No research has been done in this area. That, I suppose, would be thought too intrusive, a step into forbidden territory. One of the biggest problems is that we can never know: voiceless females cannot be researched.

Back again to the veiled lady in the park. She was pushing a baby in a pram – a girl, probably ten months old, who had on a gay orange dress and an Alice band with a pretty bow. The buggy was one of those in which the child faces the world, not the pusher. Just as well. Imagine the child looking at a face which wasn't a face, trying to connect with a mother who could not coo at her, smile, make funny faces or laugh in public. We know the tiniest babies respond to voices, facial expressions and touch. As the girl grew older, the family would, I imagine, start to define/confine her too. All over the country, younger and younger girls have headscarves on. Stretchy baby hijabs are available in London markets and some Asian and Arab shops (some of the cutest ones have false designer logos – 'Chanel' or 'Calvin Klein' are de rigueur). So this child, in all probability, would not be allowed to show her hair. Then, from the age of eight, she might be put into long-sleeved grey or brown or black gowns. Why don't they at least make the infant jilbabs red or bright green or blue? Can't have that: too much fun. The gowns impede free movement; they are an encumbrance, a lesson. The children thus clad can't play properly in playgrounds – they will trip over as they run. By the time they are teenagers, the indoctrination will be complete.

The world bursts with colour, but many of them will be dull shadows on the landscape and most will never let the wind blow through their hair. Of course, they still laugh and play and love life – but in a severely restricted environment. And they will be incessantly watched.

Saddest of all, they will not know how small their world is.

As the daughter grows up, she will plead to wear grown-up clothes for fun. In her case, she will clamour for the niqab, just like other little girls want to wear mummy's high-heeled shoes and dresses. Her mum is her role model.

Start soon enough and daughters will know their place and their fate. They will accept the self-demeaning falsehood that their gender causes disruption and must therefore submit to severe restraints for the sake of the world.

There was a son too, about four, full of smiles, running around kicking a ball, sometimes coming over to the mother and daughter, shouting about this and that in Urdu. The replies were muffled. He too will grow up thinking this is what perfect women are or should be. The mother, after all, is a boy's first female love and heroine. He will most probably expect his sister to follow suit (and will make damn sure she conforms, for that is the role of a brother) and the woman he eventually marries will again have to follow the example set by her mother-in-law. If he decides to break out, do his own thing, let his wife wear what she wishes, he will be banished from the clan. The daughter will be punished much more severely if she doesn't obey.

If children are told by people they trust that covering up is what good girls must do, that it is what Allah has commanded, that to disobey would land them in hell, then that is what they do.

I did ask one mum who wore a hijab and cloak why her tiny daughters were all in headscarves: 'I am training them so they don't mind when the time comes for jilbab.'

I carried on: 'But the Qur'an does not say cover up young girls?'

Her answer: 'It does. The Imam said so, but you have to understand it properly. I don't speak Arabic so I listen to him.'

She herself was born in the UK. Her mum, who was with her, was in a bright green, printed shalwar kameez. She clearly didn't care to follow the Imam's orders.

All faiths promote pernicious, sexist doctrines: females are sirens, morally feeble, unsafe, dirty, dangerous destabilisers, Delilahs who can deplete masculinity. Women believe these slurs and feel obliged to mitigate the harm they supposedly spread, the curses they bring to families, communities and societies.

Hinduism strictly restricts and maligns menstruating women, widows and unmarried mothers. Female foetuses are still aborted because girls are thought a burden and a blight.

In Christianity, Eve could not resist the apple offered to her by the serpent and look what happened: the expulsion of humanity from Eden was all her fault. That must be why Christians from all denominations are still opposed to women priests and bishops. Nuns have always worn severe head coverings and full gowns – their sacrifice for the God who made them female, sexual and fertile. How can it possibly be righteous to disclaim divine creation, to choose sterility and renounce the life force of desire? (Catholic clergymen also relinquish sexual relations so they can be 'pure'. Sex is a sin; women are whores or Madonnas.)

In strict Judaism, married women are required to cover their hair as a mark of fidelity and virtue. Modern Jewish women don't heed these archaic conventions but Hassidic women do still cover their hair with scarves or hats and some orthodox women wear gorgeous wigs. This could be compromise or subversion, or yet another example of religious inanity.

The venerated Egyptian author Alaa Al-Aswany wrote, in one of the most compelling commentaries on these ancient, anti-female prejudices: '[This view] is unfair and inhuman, because men and women commit sin together and the responsibility is shared and equal.'[5]

So, yes, organised religions have discriminatory rules and dreadful attitudes towards women – one half of the world. None of the other faiths, however, seem to have embarked on a fresh and zealous worldwide mission to fight progressive developments and modernity. Uniquely and frighteningly, the version of Islam that is spreading all over the world is getting more misogynistic

---

5   'When Women are Sinners in the Eyes of Extremists', *The Independent*, 28 October, 2009.

and pushing back against female egalitarianism. Muslim nations and communities are entering a new dark age. My book's focus is the veil because it represents this drift.

Unforgivably, and for cynical reasons, the British state seems to be aiding and abetting Islamicist obscurantism and ideological reach. The government wants to keep the Saudis and Qataris – both nations home to Wahabism and Salafism – as 'allies' in the 'War on Terror'. Our power brokers know these and other Islamic states (or states within states) fund ideologues and terrorists. They have infiltrated schools, homes, mosques, communities, some universities, even entire geographical areas. Their oil and wealth have captured our political classes.

In the next section, I detail several personal experiences and other examples of this sinister mission creep.

In 1972, thousands of entrepreneurial Ugandan Asians had migrated to Leicester and revived the ailing economy. Unlike some northern towns, the Midland city was cosmopolitan and cohesive. The Muslims among them – Sunni, Shia and various sub-sects – had always got on with each other and their lives. In 2005, I went up there and was told, off the record, that the Saudis had moved in and were imposing, or subtly disseminating, their own joyless, restrictive, anti-female brand of worship. Intra-Muslim tensions were showing up in schools, mosques, localities, even families. Big money, mutual suspicion and aggressive proselytising had changed the place I had once loved. One felt the prickles of animosity in the air and on the skin.

I went to see Kulsum (not her real name), an old Sunni neighbour from back in Uganda. She didn't smile when she opened the door. We had last met a year earlier and I barely recognised the woman. She had donned a jilbab and hectored me about my wicked ways, particularly my hair and lipstick. We were like sisters once, wearing the same cheap hair ornaments and earrings, cutting each other's fringes, brewing perfumes from rose and jasmine petals. Now she, in bleak grey, had apparently found the true path, and I, for sure, was going to be thrown into the pits of burning hell. Kulsum had been turned by Deobandis, another ultra-orthodox Sunni stream. I never spoke to her again. Our charming childhood story had been torn up.

21

With another day came another depressing example of how Leicester is becoming intolerant and intolerable to many. A Sunni Muslim academic who was born and raised there is moving out:

> The local councils and businesses have done so much to make this town prosperous, untroubled, and positive. Now – though they don't say it – they know some very negative forces are about and people are frightened. My wife is Shia and we have been told by some Salafi maniacs that our marriage is not valid in the eyes of God, that our kids are illegitimate. She will not cover up – I don't want her to either. So that is another black mark against us. Our daughters will never be put into those things. We have to leave to be free.

On this visit I was filming a state-funded Muslim girl's secondary school. It was run by a very charming, suave Muslim head. All the pupils were dressed in full burkha. He told me it wasn't an 'official uniform', but what the pupils and their parents wanted. This was repeated to me by the girls in two classrooms. They were like typical teenagers – loud, happy and voluble. Some even said they listened to Madonna. But the sight of them all wrapped in black made me want to weep. Why was it cool to be shrouded in black? They couldn't really explain. 'It's like, my religion, like in Islam we have to,' was the best I could get out of them. What kind of future did they have in this fast-moving, contemporary world?

I wrote to the Department for Education about my concerns. Labour was running the country; Ruth Kelly was the Secretary of State. I got no reply. Labour then pandered to Imams and unelected Muslim leaders in key seats in return for bagfuls of votes gathered, collected and delivered. Michael Gove, when he became Secretary of State, was so obsessively committed to the idea of free schools he did not think through the dangers of parent-driven religious education. Faith-based schools of all denominations should be scrapped. They constrict young minds and encourage separatism and unholy self-regard. America, that God-fearing nation, does not permit any religious practices in state-funded schools. They don't even do Christmas. The UK keenly follows American economics, foreign policies and bad food habits, but not, inexplicably, the secular national education model. By the time Gove left office, a good many of these free Muslim schools had been colonised by regressive heads and governors. Every one of them insisted on some kind of cover, thus making young girls conscious of their status and gender danger. In 2014, serious concerns were expressed by teachers and parents that religious and ordinary state schools in various parts of Britain had been infiltrated by Saudi-influenced Muslims.[6]

In some areas where hardline Imams hold sway, the headscarf is seen as risqué because it focuses attention on the face. Females who only cover their hair are thought impure and impious. Munira, the hijabi daughter of an old acquaintance, for example, was engaged to a Muslim man she had known for years. Marriage plans were cancelled after she refused to comply with

---

6   In the summer of 2014, the 'Trojan Horse' rows broke out. Allegations were made of takeovers in schools by hardline Muslims. Inspectors were sent in amid accusations of 'Islamaphobia'. I have looked into this and am convinced that governors, parents and some teachers are pushing Wahabi-based Islam in several schools around the country.

new orders from her fiancé to wear a burkha. He is a medical doctor, she a social worker.

There are now female Wahabis who are getting to Muslims around the globe. One of the most infamous and charismatic of those is Farhat Hashmi. Born in Pakistan into an educated family, she has a PhD from Glasgow University and now disseminates her 'god-given advice' on the web and in bestselling DVDs. She is fully hidden from the public eye, telling her millions of followers that men can have multiple wives, that wives must submit, and that western values must be rejected. She has opened seminaries in Canada where these prejudices are drummed into minds. Canada has tried to deport her but, last I heard, in spite of public revulsion against her teachings, they could not get her to leave. Hashmi is hugely influential in the UK and some of my sources tell me she is more so than Imams. British Pakistani families have become ardent followers.

All this is going on, and British latitudinarians still think all they have to do is tolerate customs and ways that are outside their world. This is lazy and could even be a kind of benign bigotry. I often ask them what they would say or do if their own daughters decided one day to put on the hijab or niqab? They would, of course, dissuade their girls, argue and explain what is wrong with taking up such garments. If they only knew what is happening behind closed doors and closed minds.

In 2005, while I was browsing the shops on Chiswick High Road, I became aware of a woman shadowing me, rather too close in that private space we all subconsciously carry around us. She was covered from head to toe in a black burkha. Tight, white gloves covered her hands. She wore perfume or hair oil smelling of roses. At one point, I nearly tripped over her foot and she said 'sorry' softly. I drove home and twenty minutes later the doorbell rang. I opened the door to see the woman standing there, her raven cloak billowing. Her eyes were light brown. She said nothing at first, and then asked, in perfect English, if she could come in: 'Please, please, I know who you are and I must speak to you.' She told me her name, showed me her EU passport – even though I could not match the picture with the face. She was from somewhere near Bolton. I will call her Sana.

I let her in. She took off her burkha, and there before

me was a woman so badly battered and beaten that she looked as if she had been painted in deep blue, purple and livid pink. The sides of her mouth were torn. 'My father and two brothers put fists in my mouth because I was screaming,' she explained. 'Then they forced me to wear the niqab, so no one can see what they've done.'

She is one of many such females whose rights are trampled on by those who are meant to care for them. Relatives beat up women and girls because they want them to agree to marriages or just because the girls want a little more independence, to go to college and get jobs. They know the police are getting wise to family abuse, forced marriages and 'honour' killings. So the perpetrators now get them under burkhas to conceal the evidence of their brutality.

Sana was twenty-five, and training to become a science teacher. Someone told the family they saw her talking to men at the bus stop. It was a lie, 'but this gossip can kill us'. Her father, uncle and brothers kicked and punched her to get her to confess to things she hadn't done. Then they ordered her to quit the course. When she refused, they locked her in a bedroom and carried on with the torture. She managed to escape with her passport, and a friend drove her to London. I took her to a women's refuge. As I dropped her off she said tearfully that her escape would break her mother's heart. Her mother's heart, I said, should have broken to witness what was done to her daughter. This chemistry graduate eventually remade her life, changed her name and lives far away from Bolton.

Domestic violence is an evil found in all countries, classes and communities. Most female sufferers wear concealing clothes and make-up and tell fabricated stories. The burkha or niqab is the most effective way to hide injuries. I have letters from young British Muslim wives making these allegations, all too terrified to go public. Mariyam writes: 'He says he doesn't want his name spoilt – that his honour is important. If they see what he is doing to me, his name will be spoilt.' They call these 'honour' crimes – an insult to victims.

Two days after Sana had come to the door, I heard a telling radio interview with two Saudi men, both educated in the West. They were driving around Riyadh in a flash car, talking to a reporter.

One of them, an engineer, had had a girlfriend in the US and had done all the stuff college guys do: 'Those white girls are too easy. They are all prostitutes. They show everything. Let men touch them everywhere. They thought I had money so many wanted to have sex with me. Our women, they are clean. They must be.'

The other chap chipped in, agitated, manic even: 'Look at them, see how they are walking, turning their heads. I can see their bodies. They are like prostitutes also. They should not be allowed out of the houses.'

The women he was talking about were in full niqab. I have heard similar comments from Muslim men in Tower Hamlets and northern towns. Nothing is ever going to be modest enough for them. Perhaps boxes made of light wood next so no contours or movements are visible? I don't believe so. What hard Muslim men want – really, really want – is to banish the Muslim female from all shared spaces, including mosques and malls, gardens and streets, schools and colleges, even hospitals and government buildings. They want them walled-up, kept indoors cooking and cleaning, making babies, uncomplaining, silent and grateful.

In 2011, I went to Egypt and Jordan just after the first
burst of the Arab Spring. I had been to Cairo before and
each time I visited I noticed more women were covering
up heads, bodies and faces than before. But this time,
I saw hardly any female hair. It was gone from public
view. They got rid of Mubarak and conservative values moved in. The revolution was hijacked. How had
this happened? How had it been allowed to happen?
It was, in part, the influence of the ultra-conservative
Muslim Brotherhood, which had been banned for dec-
ades and was finally able to come out and take charge in
working-class neighbourhoods. The women were also
trying to keep safe. Since the pro-democracy eruptions,
'Egypt has witnessed a large number of women being
sexually assaulted and raped – simply for daring to
take a stand. It is the shameful, untold story of an Arab
Spring revolution that went off track.'[7] Gang rapes took
place in central Cairo while the crowds watched. The
Egyptian Centre for Women's Rights claims over 80 per
cent of females in Egypt have been sexually harassed.

---

7   Angella Johnson, 'Freedom in Egypt?', *Mail on Sunday*, 7 July 2013.

Mona Eltahawy is an American-Egyptian journalist who was arrested, allegedly beaten and sexually
assaulted by police officers in Cairo in November 2011.
In a recent article she wrote: 'We have no freedom.
They hate us women. Even after these revolutions, all
is considered more or less well with the world as long
as women are covered up, anchored to the home … the
system treats half of humanity like animals.'[8]

A Christian academic told me she had started to
wear the hijab when outside the home because Cairo
had become dangerous for women.

The really terrible truth is that at the same time as
this national cover-up, assaults on girls and women
increased dramatically. Even in Tahrir Square, young
women had their clothes ripped off and were seriously
assaulted and humiliated. As were white journalists,
one of whom I spoke to as she was preparing to fly
back to Europe. She was raped in broad daylight even
though she had on a loose top and trousers and a scarf
around her head:

---

8   www.foreignpolicy.com, 23 April 2012.

Egyptian gangs go around like wolves looking for women.
The hijab and face veil cannot stop them. One woman
who was buggered was in full niqab. I found her but her
family has closed down the subject. She brought shame to
them. What? By walking around in a black sheet?

All Arab nations are bottom of the gender equality index
produced by the World Economic Forum. As Eltahawy
writes: 'Name me an Arab country and I will recite a
litany of abuses against women fuelled by a toxic mix
of religion and culture.'[9]

Liberal Turks and Arabs of various denominations
debate and argue about these trends. The same litany can be found in various Muslim communities in
this country, but Britons prefer not to deal with the
challenges, or to dismiss conservative Muslims as bar-
barians unfit to live in the West. Indolent acceptance or
racist disengagement leave the issues un-tackled. This
is neither fair nor wise.

Just three weeks after the encounter in the park, with

---

9   Ibid.

which I started this section, I went to Hammersmith hospital for a blood test. The walk-in clinic, surprisingly, had only a few patients waiting. I took a ticket from a machine and sat down. A couple came to the ticket machine. She was slight and in a full niqab, black with gold edging at the hem. He was in his late twenties, handsome, with a beard and in a dark blue suit. He pulled out a ticket and had some papers in his hand. She was called after I was done, but while I was still in the room. Both came in together and he said he would not let a man take blood samples from his wife. He asked for a female practitioner. None was available. He shouted. They told him to leave and try again another day. She said nothing, but her eyes seemed to indicate she really didn't want such scenes. But that is merely conjecture. Apparently now, some UK Muslim families object strongly to a male phlebotomist taking blood from a female arm. (Would they also insist that transfusions from 'male' blood are forbidden? Probably.)

Saudi rules, imported into Britain, are becoming entrenched. Over there, in July 2013, a mother, father and child were involved in a car accident. He died, and she needed an emergency hand amputation, which would not be done because there was no legal male guardian to authorise the procedure.

The all-powerful Commission for the Promotion of Virtue and Prevention of Vice sends out enforcers. Some of them prevented fifteen schoolgirls from being rescued in a school fire: the children were not properly covered so although the firemen tried to save them, they were stopped. The girls died.

These virtue enforcers have now banned women from going to any clinic or hospital or having any treatment without permission from, and the presence of, a male relative. One female doctor in that country described the difficulties of trying to work while fully covered, including trying to listen to heart rhythms through a black cloak or trying to treat a comatose female patient who still had to be fully veiled.[10] It doesn't end there in Saudi Arabia. It won't end here either. The autonomy of countless Muslim women, even in medical situations, is being taken away in the UK. Some are being turned into

10 *The Land of Invisible Women*, Quanta A. Ahmed, MD, Sourcebooks Inc, 2008.

perpetual minors, while others are withdrawing into metaphorical ghettos.

At four summer degree ceremonies since 2012, I have personally witnessed female Muslim students refusing to shake hands with the chancellor or vice chancellor. In one case they stood 2 feet away from him. What? Were their breaths going to lead to naughty thoughts? This was extreme discourtesy. Imagine if an EDL member had refused to shake the hand of a black chancellor? It made me feel ashamed of the sisters and the impression they gave, the discomfort they created at a time of joy and pride for themselves and the universities which had given them education and a future.

We have had cases of female Muslim medics who suddenly decide that they can't show their arms up to the elbow and therefore can't wash as they need to in order to protect patients from infections. When they applied for training, went through interviews and first started the courses, the students did not make these demands – that came later. Maybe some chose not to reveal their true religious selves until they had been accepted, but I am persuaded that they were compelled to by families

or approached and threatened by hardliners. I know
three undergraduates at London universities who were
stalked and harried by Muslim students for showing
their hair and arms.

True, there are Muslim women who seem not have
been pressured but who have decided to follow these
customs for reasons I cannot fathom. This cohort is getting more assertive and obdurate. Something or someone
has clearly got to them.

In October 2013, *Channel 4 News* showed various
young and articulate Muslim women who covered themselves completely – except, that is, for the eyes, which
burnt bright and seemed full of fervour. They spoke
from the same crib sheet. It was to do with choice, rights,
spirituality, choice, rights etc. Not one of them said they
were following a Qur'anic injunction, because there
is no such injunction. I was invited by the channel to
debate with these excitable and unbending niqabis at
an east London mosque. I did so with conviction and
without getting overemotional. To be fair, some of the
veiled ladies on the panel were also being very calm and
thoughtful. After the filming was over, a whole crowd

from the audience came for me; like angry bats they circled, screeched and tried to intimidate me. One said my clothes were 'totally un-Islamic' – whatever that means. I was wearing trousers and a blouse. Another grabbed my arm and dug her nails in. The crew and presenter were shocked. I was furious, not frightened, and asked them to back off. This deeply unpleasant episode confirmed to me that there is now a pro-veil angry brigade which expects British society to capitulate to its demands and can turn nasty if interrogated.

They have little patience with fellow citizens who have genuine misgivings about veiling. Hijabis and niqabis can be contemptuous as well as self-righteous.

OK, so let me try to understand those British-born women who really, really want to wear the hijab, jilbab, niqab, burkha, abaya and other 'Islamic' coverings. I hear their reasons: they want to be different, to be respected, not be like those 'half-naked white girls'– something you hear often in Muslim homes – and to have the freedom to be un-free. They are smart, uncompromising and have acquired a sense of entitlement. Born in the West, they have found the weaknesses and vulnerabilities at the core of free societies. They are knowingly testing the limits of liberalism and rejecting it at the same time. It is sophistry as well as a weapon.

The group I do have sympathy for are the girls and women who veil because that is the only way they can get some freedoms, education and careers. It is a small price to pay for a better future:

> Families often demand that women, and sometimes girls too, wear hijab in the belief that it is the only way decent females should appear in public ... for some Muslim women, especially present-day working-class women, the scarf opens up a mobility in public spaces otherwise denied them, making it possible for them to attend college or work away from home.[11]

That said, this ongoing dispute is no doubt a power game for some. Some influential Muslim women have

---

11 I have found this in my work as a journalist over many years. A deal has to be done by the girl or women: education in exchange for various forms of veils. See *Education Religion*, edited by Keith Watson, Routledge, 2013, which contains thoughtful and informative essays.

become skilfully evasive or employ the language of liberalism and smooth talk to justify these practices. One, for example, says: 'I mean, is this the biggest issue we face in the UK right now? I'm a bit cynical when politicians call for a national debate that has already happened many times over.'[12]

Frankly, I am very cynical when the issue is airily waved aside. These ladies know it is getting coercive out there, but determinedly deny such inconvenient truths. Or they bring up France – to them a 'fascist' state that imposes its own ways on migrants.

I agree that France is culturally arrogant. Yet I have letters from French Algerian and Moroccan schoolgirls who support the headscarf ban imposed by their state. The school uniform ruling was necessary. What do we have in this country? John Lewis now stocks hijabs in the school uniform department. Sigh. I am not suggesting the French response to these symbols is always right or fair. Sometimes it can be shockingly

---

12 'Is the Veil the Biggest Issue We Face in the UK?', *The Guardian*, 17 September 2013.

disrespectful and supremacist. In August 2014, former minister Nadine Morano, an ally of Nicolas Sarkozy, opined that to be properly French, Muslim women had a duty to wear bikinis. Such attitudes are senseless as well as loathsome. Just as brainless and loathsome as those of Muslims who say a woman has a duty to show no part of herself in public.

Jananne Al-Ani is an extraordinary visual artist. She is mixed-race, half-Iraqi, half-Irish, an insider/outsider whose work I love because it unsettles stony certainties. Some of her pictures have the same woman completely covered, with the eyes hidden, and some have her unveiled (and almost every permutation in between). Her gaze is strong, even when we can't see it. As we watch her showing her eyes, forehead, full face and hair, thighs, we are meant, I think, to understand she is the same person. But for me, she only comes into her own when there are no cloth barriers between us. We all bring our own backgrounds and deeply felt opinions to this issue.

In a recently published reference book on Islam, the entry for 'hijab' is as follows:

The most widespread current use of the Qur'anic term applies to covering as a means of separating and distinguishing women. The requirements according to traditional Muslim legal practice indicate forms of body covering as an act of modesty, so as not to exhibit one's body for public displays or as a way of being sexually suggestive. Among some Muslims, it has come to define an assertion of Muslim identity and a way of separating 'believing' Muslim women from others. In some European countries, the hijab has come to be considered as a form of exclusion and separation by Muslims and a perceived denigration of a woman's position in society. Muslim women committed to the hijab argue for it as an expression of freedom and of their right to religious expression.[13]

This necessarily dispassionate description veils stormy emotions on both sides of the argument.

Let me take you back to my mother Jena, born in 1920, orphaned at the age of nine, educated until she was fifteen, married off in her late teens to a man much older

---

13 See Nanji, op. cit.

than her – my father, an urbane gent who had lived in the UK and dressed like Graham Greene. He was an agnostic; she was a devout Shia Muslim follower of a liberal sect led by Imam Aga Khan – as am I.

My father consumed political books and was addicted to newspapers. After they were married, he got my mother to read about women in Egypt who had defied Imams, Muftis and husbands, and thrown off the veil. There was little love in my parents' marriage but they shared a passionate interest in history, justice and politics. By the time I was born, late in the marriage, most women in the worldwide congregation had revolted against the veil, encouraged, incredibly, by our Imam, an incorrigible moderniser.

Jena told me it had started quietly, with the ladies arriving outside the mosque with their hair in plaits or buns. During the actual prayers, they covered their heads with what we call 'pachelis'. However, before and after, they let the scarf drop to the shoulder so it was part of an ensemble. They were thereby making a statement: they would be humble and pious before God, but not submit to man. Those who wore saris did the same. They had collectively decided that only by being seen would they be heard. Some were attacked or confined by their husbands and mothers-in-law, remembered Jena:

> But when change is necessary, slaps and kicks don't hurt. They give you courage. When they burnt poor Noorbanu's face, we all went to the house and cursed them. Nobody spoke to them in mosque. She never covered up her burnt face. Her husband divorced her, but a good man, a widower, Shams married her. If Allah made us why should we hide and be full of shame about our arms and faces? We must be careful of how we dress because men are men and they will make eyes at us. Which is not good for our respect. But the veil does not respect us – it makes us into prisoners for what crime? We threw it off. Now these girls want them back? Like going into a grave before you have to.

When the Shah of Persia was overthrown and the Ayatollah Khomeini imposed his brutal brand of Shia Islam on Iran, Jena wept. My niece was named after the Shah's wife, Farah Diba. My mum had a picture of him and his family in her album. Our roots are in Persia. What the women of her generation had fought for, and won, were snatched away by men in black cloaks, with scary eyes and beards.

I have a different treasured picture, a still from a video sequence by Shirin Neshat, an award-winning artist who was born and raised in Iran and now lives in the US. She is a secularist, non-hijabi, who nevertheless feels emotionally and artistically connected to her heritage. She observes without comment. The photo I have is titled 'Rapture'. This image is of women on the beach, all in black, walking towards the sea. For a few moments the ladies would cool down, enjoy the feel of salty water on their skin. Mum and I used to laugh – if only someone had taken a picture after they were soaked, the cloaks clinging to their buttocks and bosoms, sensual, in spite of the shrouds.

Twenty years ago, an Iranian friend of mine burnt herself to death in Tehran because she so objected to the headscarf she was ordered to wear. Her family still won't talk about this sacrifice, this burning protest. Her sisters think she was a heretic.

In the twentieth century, Muslim women around the world resisted their subjugation by men and rejected the embedded idea of 'natural' feminine submissiveness. In the twenty-first century, resistance has given up as conformity captures territories, minds and hearts. More cunningly still in our times, it has donned the mask of rebellion.

This then is what I see, think, hear and fear.

In the next part, I briefly cover the history of veiling and look at various contemporary uses. The Muslim world progresses then regresses, advances and reverts. It cannot develop if it keeps sliding back. The veil is a potent symbol of this dismal tendency.

Part II

Cycles of enlightenment and darkness from the past to the present

IN THE BEGINNING were the revelations. Let us go back to 610 CE, to Mecca. Muhammad, orphaned when a young boy, was married to Khadijeh, who was fifteen years older than him and a successful merchant. He had been sent by his uncle to work for her. She, a rich widow, was so impressed with the young man's honesty and hard work that she proposed marriage. This would not happen today when male–female roles in Muslim families are so much more rigid than they were back then.

One day, Muhammad was meditating, reflecting on life, truths and morality in a cave near Mecca. He often retreated to this tranquil cavern in the hills. In the quiet of the cave, the archangel Gabriel appeared before him and got him to recite the first words sent by God. Several other such encounters and messages followed. The Qur'an is a written record of those divine missives. All other revered texts are written by men, some which are believed to be the sayings of the Prophet, while the rest are legal pronouncements or interpretations of the original holy tome. None are written by women.

This revealed religion then spread across most parts of the world, sometimes peacefully, sometimes through conquest. Today Islam is gaining more converts than any other faith, particularly in the West.

I am not going into all the theological disputes and schisms that followed the death of the Prophet in 632 CE. I am not qualified to do that and, in any case, there is no agreement between various and opposing doctrines. For the purposes of this book, I do, however, need to highlight some basics. I can't speak or

write Arabic so I depend on unbiased scholars who
do. These passages in the Qur'an[14] mention body
coverings:

> There will be a veil between them [the inmates of para-
> dise] and residents of hell.

> [To those of you who don't listen], our hearts are
> immured against what you call us to. There is a deaf-
> ness in our ears and a veil lies between us.

> Oh you who believe, do not enter the houses of the
> Prophet for a meal without awaiting the proper time,
> unless asked, and enter when you are invited. Depart
> when you have eaten and don't stay on talking. This
> puts the Prophet to inconvenience and he feels embar-
> rassed in saying the truth. And when you ask his wife
> for something of utility, ask for it from behind a screen.
> This is for the purity of your hearts and theirs.

---

14 I have used the Qu'ran translated by Ahmed Ali, Princeton, 2001, through-
out this book.

Sahar Amer, associate professor at the University of North Carolina, Chapel Hill, reflects on these parts of the holy book: 'It is evident to anyone reading these passages that, except for the last quotation, the word "hijab", though used in the Arabic text, is not understood to mean or refer in any way to an Islamic dress code for women.'

To me, most of the time, the veil is used metaphorically, at times lyrically. The third passage can be, and has been, invoked by those who believe the veil is an inviolable, religious duty.[15]

Three further paragraphs do directly address modesty in dress and behaviour.

> Tell the believing men to lower their eyes and guard their
> private parts. God is aware of what they do. Tell the
> believing women to lower their eyes, guard their private
> parts and not display their charms except what is appar-
> ent outwardly and to cover their bosoms with their veils
> and not show their finery except to their husbands or

---

15 I am indebted to Sahar Amer of the University of North Carolina, Chapel Hill, for helping me understand what the Qu'ran says on the veil. She delivered a talk on this in 2000 at an education conference. It can be read online.

their fathers, or fathers-in-law, or their sons, brothers, or stepsons, brothers' and sisters' sons, or their women attendants or captives, or male attendants who do not have any need (for women), or boys not yet aware of sex. They should not walk stamping their feet lest they make known what they hide of their ornaments.

Oh wives of the Prophet, you are not like other women … stay at home and do not deck yourselves with ostentation in these days of paganism; fulfil your devotional obligations, pay the zakat [alms], and obey God and His Apostles.

Oh Prophet, tell your wives and daughters and women of the faithful, to draw their wraps a little over them. They will thus be recognised and no harm will come to them. God is forgiving and kind.

Amer ruminates on these paragraphs:

[Nowhere] is hijab used to describe, let alone to prescribe, the necessity for Muslim women to wear a headscarf or any of the other pieces of clothing often seen covering women in Islamic countries today. Even after reading these passages dealing with the female dress code, one continues to wonder what exactly the hijab is: is it supposed to be a simple scarf? A purdah? A chador? Or something else? Which parts of the body exactly is it supposed to cover: just the hair? The hair and the neck? The arms? Hands? Feet? Face? Eyes? What colour is it supposed to be?[16]

The great variations indicate that these customs are determined not by the eternal edicts of Islam but cultures, geographies and histories.

More importantly still, the only women expected to be completely covered

in the early days of Islam were the wives of the Prophet Muhammad, known in the Qur'an as 'the mothers of the believers'. Their role was to serve as the spiritual matrons of the Muslim community and, as a result, they were

16 Ibid.

required to live and dress differently from other women
to designate their status.[17]

And to protect themselves. Paganism was still strong
among many powerful tribes, and battles were raging
between Muslims and those who rebuffed the Prophet
and his messages. He had many enemies and some of
them taunted the women, sullied their names, ogled at
and insulted them. To keep them safe and sane, they were
commanded to speak to men 'through a curtain'. Inevi-
tably, as the female custodians of the faith began to cover
themselves, they started a trend. Rich ladies wanted to
imitate the elite religious family and identify themselves as
special, superior to the hoi polloi. Hidden behind sheaths,
they could avoid mendicants and petitioners. It was not
piety but vanity and snobbery that made them do it.

Furthermore, in the one section that dwells on respect-
ability and modesty, men are asked to be just as restrained
as women. The words used for men are the same as those

---

17 Reputable scholars and commentators agree that this special duty was placed
    on the women in the Prophet's household. See 'Lifting the Veil on the Debate
    over Veils', Kamran Pasha, *Huffington Post*, 2011.

used for women. Men pay no heed to those commands and instead exert patriarchal control over every aspect of female life from cradle to grave.

Abu Bakr, an early convert, proselytised and fought wars in the name of Islam, provided funds for the cause, and, to mark the trust between them, arranged a marriage between his young daughter, Aisha, and Muhammad. Following the death of the Prophet, Abu Bakr became the first ever Caliph, leader of Muslims. Aisha led armies against those who rejected Abu Bakr's claims and instead supported Ali (married to Fatima, the Prophet's eldest daughter – another strong leading lady). Women then could be fiercely independent.

The granddaughter of Abu Bakr, named Aisha bint Talha, told the second of her three husbands that she would never wear the veil: 'Since God, the Exalted has put upon me the stamp of beauty, it is my wish that the public should view that beauty and thereby recognise His grace unto them. I will not veil. No one can force me to do anything.'[18]

---

18 Kadri, op. cit., p. 29.

All that has been forgotten, erased from collective memory. Fatema Mernissi, a renowned Algerian post-colonialist feminist explains the various, original meanings of 'hijab' and social control mechanisms:

> [The concept] is three-dimensional and these dimensions often cut across each other. The first is a visual dimension: hiding from view. The root of the verb *hajaba* means to 'hide'. The second dimension is spatial: to separate, to mark a boundary, establish a threshold. Lastly the third dimension is ethical: it relates to the question of prohibition. At this level we are dealing not with tangible categories which exist in the reality of the senses, such as the visual or the spatial, but with the abstract reality that is the order of ideas. A space hidden by hijab is a forbidden space.[19]

In other words, it is a barrier that keeps women from public participation. From being a protective measure

---

19 *Women's Rebellion and Islamic Memory*, Fatema Mernissi, Zed Books, 1996, pp. 51–52.

for the Prophet's women, it has become a symbol of women accepting they are a source of disorder. Women cannot be active and equal citizens if they accept this deal, this characterisation.

Many do defy these pernicious assumptions and expectations, at great cost to themselves. They find themselves defenceless because they have 'ventured into areas that are not theirs ... Walking about freely with face uncovered is exhibiting oneself',[20] asking for it, because poor men cannot fight such terrible temptations. This is why victims of rape are held as responsible for the crime as their assailants – in my view, one of the most unjust and unfair presumptions of all. This guilt of being female, even when attacked, is not confined to Muslims. It is found in all eastern countries and religions. However, in Muslim societies, the brutalisation and injustice is getting worse and redress is denied.

Muslim women who choose to cover up, and their defenders too, do not confront male hypocrisy or lust.

---

20 *Islam and Democracy*, Fatima Mernissi, Virago Press, 1993, pp. 7–8.

They let men off the hook and take all responsibility for probity. Additionally, they have created their own myths around the veil or have come to see it as part of the struggle against western might, hubris and greed. I really don't believe I must wear some kind of modesty cloth to fight effectively for the rights of fellow Muslims, or other citizens who also suffer deprivation and discrimination, or abhor iniquitous British foreign policies and double standards.

Other facts are neatly sidestepped by those Muslims who claim the veil for Islam: 'It originated from ancient Indo-European cultures such as the Hittites, Greeks, Romans and Persians. It was also practised by the Assyrians … women in medieval Europe dressed more like women in the Muslim world than is realised.'[21]

The Greek philosopher Strabo, writing in the first century CE, noted that some Persian women were fully veiled,[22] and Tertullian, a third-century Christian,

---

21 See: 'Some Thoughts on the Veil', Max Dashu; it is a thought-provoking essay on the politics of the veil.

22 *Geographica* III, Strabo.

described Arab women who covered their faces as well as their bodies, approving of the discipline of the veil and denouncing women who rebelled against its enforcement.[23]

During the early ages of Judaism, a woman could be fined if she ventured out without being properly covered. Upper-class Byzantine, Christian, Zoroastrian and Greek ladies also concealed their faces and bodies, and poorer women could be punished for covering up in some of those old civilizations – they had to be prevented from getting above themselves. Assyrian kings expected the females they owned, or were related to, to shield themselves from the eyes of men outside the clan. This was sexual jealousy as well as a way of making sure bloodlines were never in danger of being polluted.

In old paintings from those places and times, you see gowns buttoned right up to the neck, hair hidden under a scarf and inner cap (much like the hijabis we see today) or turbans. For the wealthier women,

---

23 *On the Veiling of Virgins*, III, Tertullian.

sequestering themselves behind luxurious fabrics 'was a sign of high status and nobility, while women who were unveiled were denigrated as low class and, indeed, prostitutes would go about unveiled as a means of advertising their wares. "Respectable" Christian women believed that showing their beauty to all and sundry was cheap and demeaning.'[24]

Some scholars claim that the warriors of Islam were offended by the social hierarchies they found in Zoroastrian and Christian states:

[Egalitarian] Muslim leaders began to encourage veiling across every social spectrum to neutralise the pretensions of the aristocracy. So the mass introduction of veiling in the Middle East was originally an effort at elevating the lower classes and defusing the privileges of the wealthy. While hard to imagine today, the veil was actually a tool of social progress in a world with very different values.[25]

---

24 Pasha, op. cit.

25 Ibid.

To this day, headscarves are worn by Sikhs, Hindus, traditional Greeks, Catholics and others. They do so because that is a cultural demand or out of choice. But only Muslims are imposing ever more restrictions on female clothing.

Veils predate Islam and were adopted by early Muslims for various reasons; today's revivalists not only claim these garments for Islam, they do so to silence women.

They detest women like me or Mernissi, who won't be good and quiet and obliging. She asks: 'Why don't our politicians appreciate our hairdos, our bare faces and our direct looks? Why do [powerful Muslim men] all dream of this fully veiled, self-deprecating creature?'

More disturbingly, I wonder why so many Muslim women and girls submit to the dehumanisation and erasure? There have been times in history when they did not do so, while still being devout Muslims.

Contemporary scholars, Ziauddin Sardar and Zafar Abbas Malik, make these unusually candid statements in their clear and useful book, *Introducing Islam*:

Traditional Muslim thought has been very unkind and oppressive to women. While religious scholars constantly recite the list of women's rights in Islam, they have been undermining those very rights for centuries. While Qur'anic injunctions are always directed towards the 'believing men' and the 'believing women' their interpretations conveniently forget the men and place all the burden on women … 'Modest' and decent behaviour for women in public has been interpreted as a rigid dress code, despite the openness and much wider significance of the Qur'anic verses and their deliberate vagueness which are meant to allow the time-bound changes that are necessary for social and moral growth of society. In a total perversion of the Qur'anic advice, dressing modestly has thus been interpreted as dressing like a nun, covered from head to foot, showing only a woman's face (in some circles only the eyes), wrists and feet. An injunction meant to liberate from the oppressions of 'beauty' and 'fashion' ends up as an instrument of oppression.[26]

---

26 *Introducing Islam*, Ziauddin Sardar and Zafar Abbas Malik, Icon Books, 1994, p. 160.

Colonialism and liberation

So, in sum, the veil has been many things to many people: a symbol of wealth and class; a garment to protect female integrity; a statement of religious devoutness; a marker of male ownership; at times, a cultural definer. During the colonial period, the years of struggle for independence, and the post-colonial era, it became a politicised and polarising emblem. (As it has been again since the 9/11 attacks.)

Whatever European revisionists claim, colonialism exploited and impoverished the subjugated, left their countries and borders in a mess and vandalised existing systems and connections. It also took away the pride and will of those it controlled. As David Cameron accepted in Pakistan in 2011, many of the most intractable problems around the world today can be traced back to British colonialism.

However, too many Muslims play this blame game, which only infantilises them. Some deep-seated problems are caused by internal factors, not old occupiers or external agents. Colonialism always was, and is today, used as an alibi by those who cannot admit to Muslim culpability.

Across Arabia, Christian missionaries and some of the

most unsavoury, supercilious representatives of the colonial nations condemned the treatment and dress codes of Muslim females. Lord Cromer was the all-powerful controller of Egypt from 1883 to 1907; he declared that gender segregation and seclusion had a 'baneful effect on eastern society' and that Arabs were being held back because their women had no equality in the home, mosques or society. In India, Thomas Macaulay and others from the ruling classes insisted western civilisation had to be imposed in order to move the natives on. Such men held that there was a hierarchy of races and cultures. They were arrogant and racist. But on the rights of women, the detestable Cromer was right: 'the fatal obstacle' to Egypt's development was indeed the position of women. His education policies were detrimental to girls and women, so he was also a hypocrite – but he was right about the veil. It was indeed an impediment to community and national progress.

But even back then, those who opposed occupation could not allow themselves to admit to this sorry reality. Instead, the intellectual response was that the veil was an irrelevance, or in the domestic domain and therefore not the business of outsiders. They wanted instead the focus to be on education and participation, clearly both fundamental to female progress and easier to deal with than the controversial veil.

Many of those fighting white rule went even further. They felt honour-bound to oppose imperialist concerns and so defend female invisibility and seclusion. Psychoanalyst Franz Fanon, a Martiniquan, was a great anti-colonial intellectual; his writings about the French in Algeria profoundly affected me when I was at university in Uganda. So when he wrote this, I too was carried away by the prose and the passion: 'The veil was a mechanism of resistance but its value for the social group remained very strong ... the veil was worn because the occupier was bent on unveiling Algeria.' And yes, it is true that French commanders forced Arab women to unveil. It was violation, deliberate humiliation. That old classic *The Battle of Algiers* (1966) still stirs deep feelings in Muslim audiences. But unquestioned, flatly accepted or imposed veiling is also a violation, humiliation. I had to learn that. These matters are not simple.

In the second half of the nineteenth century, intellectuals

and activists across the Muslim world began to speak up against the veil, which they saw as a symbol of patriarchal control.

In 1899, a book was published in Arabic which shook up the Middle East. Titled *The Liberation of Women*, it was by a man, Qasim Amin – an Egyptian who believed fervently that freedom, education and autonomy for females were essential for the social and political transformations sorely needed in the Muslim world. He opposed all forms of veiling and was the John Stuart Mill of his nation, region and times. Mill's treatise on the subjugation of women, published in 1869, called for females to have the same legal rights as men. Only then, according to Mill, would there be social stability and happiness for all.

Amin was vilified, and still is, even by some of our most respected Muslim intellectuals. One of them is Leila Ahmed, an Egyptian-American professor at Harvard Divinity School and brilliant scholar, whose earlier work I think was groundbreaking and profoundly influential, though I disagree with some of her more recent arguments: 'Those ideas were interjected into the native discourse as Muslim men exposed to European ideas began to reproduce and react to them, and more pervasively and insistently ... introduced and disseminated them.'

She claims Amin, a 'French, educated lawyer' was a sell-out or a Cromer stooge, that he 'rearticulated in native, upper-middle-class voice, the voice of a class economically allied with the colonisers and already adopting their lifestyles'.[27] I think he was brave and completely right. The veil was not just a harmless and/or essential form of self-identification, but a significant obstacle to the true liberation and development of females and the nation. Amin understood the perils of defending traditions simply because they were eastern or precious to the colonised. I also take issue with Ahmed's unsustainable position that ideas can be held within boundaries. They can't. Democracy, the system so many Arabs came out for in 2011, is western; so are computers, telephones and the UN Human Rights Charter.

---

27 'The Discourse of the Veil', in *Veil*, ed. David Bailey and Gilane Tawadros, Institute of International Visual Arts, p. 48.

Let me reiterate some vital points: Islamic nations are not among the most productive nations. Colonial carve-ups and games are responsible for that, and so too are the failures of successive post-colonial governments. None of them embedded the rights of women, real democracy or free thought.

It was tried. What I am about to write will whip up yet more stormy controversies, for many of those who did push to change macho Muslim societies have, since their heyday, come to be despised and accused of that crime 'westernisation'.

In around 1909, Iranian women – middle-class and assertive – set up secret societies to fight for better gender equality. Some were exposed, attacked, had their houses burnt down. Nevertheless, in 1919, a women's magazine was started in Iran by a journalist, Sediqeh Dowlatabadi. It was called *Zaban-e Zanan* (*Voice of Women*), and it totally opposed the veil. A year later, a new magazine, *Nameh-ye banovan* (*Women's Letter*), aimed to 'awaken suffering Iranian women'. It too was against the veil. These women were not colonialism's handmaidens. They fought for their sisters and wanted them to move out of emotional and social ghettos. Their legacy has been crushed by men and squandered by too many women in their country.

Huda Sha'arawi, a heroine to my mother, set up the Egyptian Women's Union in the early '20s. One day in 1923, disembarking from a train at Cairo central station, in full view of all who were there, she threw off her face veil. She had resented these rules and the seclusion of females. Her husband was dead. She was free. She had just been to the international suffrage alliance congress in Rome and that had strengthened her will. Though other Arab feminists thought this was unnecessary provocation, that the priorities should be education and representation, she, like Amin, understood these clothes were an impediment to those aspirations. She was upper class and wealthy and so could defy the norms. She did it not because she could, but because she understood that feminism was not only about 'choice', but real, open equality. In these times, she has been written off as irrelevant and a cultural traitor.

So too was the last Shah of Iran, Reza Pahlavi. He ruled Iran between 1941 and 1979, until revolutionaries loyal to the Ayatollah Khomeini overthrew him and established the Islamic Republic. The Shah was a placeman, puppet of the US and UK, worst of all a despot. He tolerated no dissent, was often heartless and overly grandiose. But that was not all he was. There was another side to him, now forgotten. He was a moderniser, keen on freeing up the women so they could be confidently themselves and have careers. He got them into schools and universities, and provided grants to those from poor families so they could travel abroad. (In the Qur'an, Muslim men and women are asked to go as far as China to seek out knowledge.) Women were also given the vote, equal shares in property and custody rights after divorce. But he got them to unveil, using his police and special secret service to push his will on all matters, and so he became a hate figure. Of course it was hard for the women to give up their protective tents, and enforced unveiling is gravely intrusive, but they were on the road to some kind of parity with men when the Shah was deposed.

The Ayatollah Khomeini unseated him, and what happened? Millions feel more oppressed today than they did under the Shah. That state protects no human rights, imprisons and executes citizens at will, terrorises its people. Women's rights are severely limited – though they can still get a good education. Those who hated the western clothes that were worn by the middle classes must be happy that females have to wear chador and scarves, and are lashed and incarcerated if they don't.

In August 2014, the Iranian regime displayed its ignominious misogyny to the whole world. Maryam Mirzakhani, born and raised in Iran, is a professor of mathematics at Stanford University and became the first woman ever to win the Fields Medal (the equivalent of the Nobel Prize in maths). She does not wear hijab, but Iranian newspapers digitally altered her image and gave her a headscarf. Is this what women wanted after the revolution?

Turkey has gone through a similar trajectory. Mustafa Kemal Atatürk came to power in Turkey in 1923. The First World War had been followed by the fall of the Ottoman Empire. The old world was gone. Atatürk was, again, a ruthless leader who fast-tracked secularism and westernisation without due concern for how his people felt about the reforms. He was totally opposed to the veil: 'In some places, I have seen women who put a piece of cloth or towel or something like that over their heads to hide their faces and who turn their backs or huddle on the ground when men pass them. What are the meanings, the sense in this behaviour?'[28] Under him, Turkey was transformed. The old Ottoman Empire, considered an enemy of the Christian world, rebranded itself as a cultural conciliator, a bridge between East and West.

When I first went to Turkey in the '70s, Atatürk was revered. It was illegal to say anything negative about him, but in most urban areas he seemed to be genuinely admired. Women were educated, fast-streamed into high-level jobs, aspirations blossomed. But, like the Shah, he was too impatient, too arrogant and autocratic. His guards ruthlessly imposed a no-veil law. Today, an Islamic government has pushed back all those reforms. Headscarves were forbidden in public places; now they are worn everywhere, signalling a rejection of the secular state.

Turkey, held up as the model 'moderate' Muslim

---

28 Quoted in Ahmed, *Veil*, op. cit. p. 51.

nation, is today fast becoming yet another constricted Islamic state. In July 2014, during Eid celebrations marking the end of the long fasting month of Ramadhan, the deputy PM, Bülent Arınç, opined he was very concerned about 'moral corruption' and 'degeneration in society'. He then made the pronouncement: 'Chastity is so important. It's not just a word. It is an ornament [for women]. A woman should be chaste. She should know the difference between public and private. She should not laugh in public.'

This is a country where almost half the women have suffered some form of domestic violence. This is what the veil is about: to keep women invisible and unable to share happiness or sadness with those outside a tight, often suffocating circle. It is not about integrity or autonomy, safety or spirituality. If niqabis can't see the connection between their coverings and the attitudes expressed by the Turkish deputy PM, then they are being willfully ignorant. And ignorance is not bliss – it is extreme folly.

Post-colonial, secular Egyptian, Tunisian and Iraqi leaders were just as zealous about getting women to shed their obedience and inhibitions so they could reach their potential. Though it is treasonable to say so, under Saddam Hussein women were free to dress as they wished, to dream and achieve what they wanted. In Egypt, after the massive defeat in the war with Israel and ensuing humiliation, conservative religious forces did gain ground, but not in the cities.

Now that reactionaries have rejected progressive politics, all these nations are economically static, violent, overpopulated, under-educated, losing their best people to the West, and institutionally sexist. In Afghanistan, Pakistan and across Muslim-run territories, Muslim women are more disadvantaged than the women were in the Prophet's life.

The voices attacking post-imperial reformers need to explain to themselves and others just what has been gained by the revivals of conservative 'Islamic' practices, by re-veiling and reverting to old, oppressive ways.

Veils are once again politicised and polarising emblems. It is also true, and deeply unfair, that for westerners, the veiled woman has become an acceptable hate figure. We must be able to debate the custom

and oppose it civilly. It is not OK, ever, to hate someone, anyone, because they are dressed the way they are.
I myself can get too overwrought when I see a veiled
Muslim woman, as I did with the mum in the park.
That is not only wrong, but counterproductive. If these
women are upset and scared off by overt hostility, they
will stay indoors, which is what their men want.

Across the Muslim world, some form of body covering appears to have become mandatory for females,
from very young to very old. In a few countries, the
codes are legally enforced while in communities around
the world, strict social customs are meekly followed
or ruthlessly imposed. In 2007, a Canadian father and
brother murdered Aqsa Parvez because she would
not cover her hair, body or face. In that same year,
Zil-e-Huma Usman, the minister for social welfare in
Pakistan, was gunned down because she did not wear
a headscarf. She was doing a tremendous amount for
the deprived and they took her life. All over Tehran, posters send out menacing messages to women
– many of whom, after years of oppression, are letting some hair show. One poster says: 'Bad hijab is

equal to prostitution. Lack of hijab means lack of man's manhood.'

In 2008 in Basra, according to Robert Fisk, more than fifteen women a month were being killed for refusing the veil.[29] In Iran, Saudi Arabia, Afghanistan and parts of Africa, women are flogged if they show forbidden flesh or hair. We see those prisoners in blue chadors in Afghanistan, with their eyes behind woven bars. In Bangladesh, hardliners are abusing and beating up Muslim women in saris – their traditional dress. Even in Palestine, where once women hardy ever covered up, it has become the norm. Girls who defy those orders are beaten up or killed. In August 2014, female Pakistani singers celebrating independence day were damned by Imams who pronounced they were sinners for singing and showing their hair.

Here and now, in some of our northern towns, families refuse to let small girls go to school without jilbabs and hijabs. Teachers allow these impositions for the sake of the children and because they do not want to upset

---

29 'The Crime that Shames the World', *The Independent*, 7 September 2010.

families. In Bradford in 2005, I was in a cab with a driver who got out, shouted at and slapped young girls because they had knee-length school uniform skirts on instead of trousers. He didn't know them, but said it was his duty to teach them how to be good Muslims.

Muslim women escaped such regimes to come to the West where they could live as free citizens. Now they find the oppression has followed them and, worse, is adopted by western Muslim females. Imagine the sense of betrayal, the bewilderment.

Present-day followers of the veil will not be challenged on these thorny details perhaps because they might then have to think about what they do. (Thinking is so much more taxing than simply following instructions.) And so you get Qahera, a veiled webcomic super-heroine, created by Deena Mohamed, a nineteen-year-old Egyptian graphic designer. The character fights misogyny and Islamaphobia, and is so thoroughly wrapped-up she could be a poster girl for the Taliban.[30] Maybe I just don't get it, but how does Qahera fight

---

30 See: qaherathesuperhero.com and *New Internationalist*, July/August 2014.

male domination by wearing garb which reinforces age-old chauvinisms? And is this costume supposed to be a provocation to western people, a way of saying 'hate me if you dare'? This is no different to claiming Barbie is a perfect icon for new feminism.

Many smart, young hijabis tell me they have escaped the tyranny of fashion, the terrible pressures faced by young women who are made to feel they are not thin enough, not sexy, not trendy, not desirable. Humera, a hijabi, spoke for many: 'We can be judged for what we say and think, not how we look. We are not always worrying about how men and other women will see us. We are really free.'

I too used to think that maybe to be thus covered means you never have a bad hair day or anxieties about spotty faces; that you never have to ask, 'Does my bum look big in this?'

Not so, not at all. Manijeh, a very dear friend who died too young of cancer, was an Iranian who had settled in London after the Ayatollah swept into power. She loved fashion and make-up, jewellery and high heels, and despised hijabi spin:

Yes, that is what they say. But you think they are not showing off under their clothes? In fact it is worse. When women get together in Tehran, they are comparing their designer clothes, bodies, skin, judging, trying to outdo each other. They even stupidly compete over shampoo and hair products. It is worse. Because outside they can't display their clothes, they become totally obsessed.

Saudi Arabian and Gulf women too are as caught up in the consumer culture as western women, only in their case it becomes claustrophobic, internalised and bitchy, even more bitchy than it is among fashionistas in the West. You can see why. Their personalities cannot be expressed in public spaces, talents are suppressed, anonymity and obedience are the only options. Within the private sphere they focus obsessively on their appearance, their sex appeal, for that is all they have been reduced to.

In 2001, research by Traci Mann, then an assistant professor of health psychology at the University of California, LA, carried out a study to find out if women living in Iran were less prone to dysmorphia, anorexia and bulimia than Iranian women living in the West. The comparison was between cohorts of students. Mann found that unhealthy obsessions about body shape and size were common in both groups, but that the students in Iran were more anxious: '[Those participants] were more likely to desire an empty stomach, more likely to vigorously exercise to control their weight or shape, less satisfied with their body size.'[31]

In 2012, I spent a morning in Harley Street watching fully veiled women, and also those in Iranian chadors, going into and coming out of plastic surgery clinics. I talked to some of the nurses and clinicians. Muslim women from the most conservative countries such as Saudi Arabia and Kuwait, I was told, were among their most frequent clients, some coming back again and again to get the perfect breasts, liposuction to flatten their stomachs, face reshapes and lifts. The women themselves were wary of me, but three did say they were there to get some beauty work done. They had to work hard to keep their men from wanting new wives.

---

31 'Which is the Perfect Body?', *Sunday Telegraph*, 25 November 2001.

I was once invited to a hair removal party by a group of rich Bahraini and Kuwaiti women. Pubic and other body hair is pulled off by millions of Muslim women using a special paste made with sugar and lemon. They often make a day of it, get together in one of their homes, eat, drink tea, gossip and pull off each other's hair. I agreed only to having my armpits and legs done – it hurt like hell. I refused, though, to let them near my private parts, even though they said some Imam or other had ordered the removal of pubic hair many centuries back. There was much dirty talk about how to please your man in bed, and oil massages, perfuming and preening. Two young, newlywed, hennaed women then had the oudh treatment – they sat naked on a stool with a hole over a small brazier which had frankincense slowly burning and letting off a strong scent. They were smoking their insides with fragrance. No hen night can match the sex banter I heard that day, but I concede they were having fun in a women-only enclave – just as those kept in harems did. Muslim men and women spend an inordinate amount of time thinking, talking, regulating and worrying about sex.

There is one more controversial aspect to consider. Veils are also erotic, always were. One of my favourite old Indian films is called *Chaudavin ka Chand* (*The Full Moon*). It is a farce and a romance in an Indian city in the '40s. The veil drives men mad, pulls them and destroys them. Women use it to flirt and seduce. That may be happening here today too, thinks Pasha:

> Why do Muslim women in free and open societies choose to don the veil. Certainly for some it is the result of social pressure from their families ... [but for many, including converts] the veil has become the ultimate symbol of feminine coyness that activates masculine desire, the quest for the hidden pearl that sparks the dance of Eros. For some women throughout history, the veil has been a symbol of femininity on a deeply primordial level.[32]

I have had letters from men, both white and Muslim, who fantasise about wanting to unwrap the veiled one,

---

32 Pasha, op. cit.

deflower her and be the only one to touch her. A young Muslim woman at Leicester University told me on camera that this was her fantasy too – she was a pearl in an oyster to be opened by one man and only him.

'What if he wants an entire necklace of pearls?' I asked.

'Well, as a Muslim woman I must accept that. But they must all be pure women like me.'

I think a bit of me died that day.

All that talk about veils making women less obsessed with bodies and more spiritual and independent – it's all bunkum. Ahmed, in her new book on the veil, wanted to find out: 'Why, after nearly disappearing from many Middle Eastern and Muslim-majority societies, had it made a comeback, and how had it spread with such swiftness?'[33] She concludes this is a 'quiet revolution' and that this manifestation of contemporary Islam is part of a positive move towards assertiveness, a way of gaining autonomy, and defining a new Muslim

---

33 *A Quiet Revolution*, Yale University Press, 2011, p. 8. The book concludes the veil is a symbol of political activism and human rights.

feminism. Though I admire the erudition and tolerance of Dr Ahmed, I conclude the opposite.

Part III

Why the veil should be repudiated

IN THE GLOBAL village, ideas, practices and policies cannot be kept within borders. In this section, I focus mostly on the UK, though I do refer to other countries and realities. My arguments rest on this premise: all of us in are in it together. We cannot be islands within islands.

But first, that question: should we outlaw veils?

No. Bans are cudgels. They punish or frighten veiled Muslim women or, worse, criminalise them, as in France. That would be deeply unjust and a violation. However, laissez-faire is either apathy or surrender – both forms of inexcusable disengagement.

There is a third way, and Birmingham College above was a good example. I think it is perfectly fair and civilized to insist on dress codes that apply to all citizens in schools and other public service establishments, and, within limits,[34] the private sector too. In broadly liberal societies, restrictions are imposed for the greater good. Nudists cannot walk our streets with impunity, and women would not be allowed to work in a bank dressed like lap dancers or nuns. What Muslim females wear as they walk on streets or in parks and shared spaces is their business. Whatever I thought and felt about that mum in the park, she was entitled to be left in peace and go about her business. But when talking to teachers in school, or cashiers in the bank, she must be obliged to show her face. It is a difficult distinction and a tough call – but one that must now be made.

This issue cannot be left to Muslims to debate and decide. British citizens from all backgrounds have a stake in what is happening. (After all, conservative

---

34 It would, for example, be unreasonable to ask customers to unveil in shops, but shops and businesses should be able to have reasonable codes for their workers.

Muslims openly scorn western women who dress brazenly, and in their faith-based schools no child would be allowed to wear a skirt that didn't go to the calves or feet. Respect is demanded, not given.) Liberal Muslims would dearly like institutions and key individuals to take a stand on their behalf. Not to do so betrays vulnerable British citizens and the nation's most cherished principles, including liberalism. Worst of all, silence encourages Islam to move back even faster into the past instead of reforming itself to meet the future.

Within reason, some concessions can be made for British Muslims for whom the veil has become a test of acceptance – for example, permitting trousers instead of skirts, as is the case in most schools. Headscarves can be accommodated, but only for adult women – not for children. I would extend this rule to include Hassidic Jewish children and Sikh boys who turn up in top knots or mini turbans.

For many of us secular Muslims, hijabs concede that parts of a woman's body need to be hidden, that females are a sexual menace or in perpetual danger from males, all of whom are presumed to be predatory. Scarves are so widely worn now that we who object must compromise. At least some women are making them colourful and beautiful. Many of them would not be allowed into post-school education and employment if they showed their hair, so on this, they win. I will, however, continue to contest the idea that hair, if shown, is a sign of wantonness.

Encouragingly, scarved and cloaked women have found smart ways to subvert that prejudice. Creative hijabis turn scarves and gowns into beautiful fashions. Some of the best beauty blogs are by hijabis.[35] They really know how to make the face alluring and defiant. Jewellery too has become a mark of individuality and style. Sometimes the head is covered but feet are in killer heels and clothes tight-fitting. I find that awesome, even though it is a little hypocritical.

It is time to reclaim the right to openly talk about these garments and assert that it is not ungodly, imperialist, 'Islamaphobic' or self-loathsome to make the case against various forms of the veil.

---

35 See for example, Sanna @lookamillion and www.prettynotincluded.com.

Here are my main arguments:

Resisting Wahabism

Rigid, radical Muslim clerics and their backers are competing to gain control of, and stamp out, the diversities of worship and practice around the world, including here in Britain. In cities with Muslim populations, Shias are maligned, mosques are becoming factional and fractious, and inhabitants of various backgrounds have become wary and uneasy. We must get our government to watch and rein in Wahabis, Deobandis and Salafis – representing the three schools of reactionary Islam. Concerned British citizens of all backgrounds should put pressure on their MPs. British governments have too long been overfriendly with Saudi Arabia and some Gulf states. These nations are indoctrinating Muslims into unacceptable submission, and implicitly encouraging anti-West hatreds.[36]

---

36 'To Really Combat Terror End Support for Saudi Arabia', Owen Jones, *The Guardian*, 1 September 2014.

A cover for sexism and sexual violence

Muslim reactionaries are obsessed with women's bodies. Females to them are 'only bodies, instruments for either legitimate pleasure or temptation, as well as factories for producing children'.[37] The appallingly high number of cases of child exploitation by Pakistani Muslim men in Rotherham and elsewhere comes from these sick attitudes. Veils are often defended as a protective measure, a way of preventing molestation. That should mean there is no rape or sexual violence in Saudi Arabia or Iran, where some form of female covering is legally enforced. Rape and sexual violence are, in fact, rife in the two countries, and within Asian families in Britain. Ruzwana Bashir, a British Muslim woman, broke all barriers, became president of the Oxford Union and is now a company CEO. She was born and raised in Skipton, in the north of England, in a traditional Muslim family. There, she was abused by a neighbour from the age of ten, a man from her community. When, as an adult, she went to the police, her family were furious with her:

---

37 Alaa Al-Aswany, *The Independent*, op. cit.

'sexual abuse has been systematically under-reported among Asian girls due to entrenched cultural taboos.'[38] This means that the abuse is kept hidden. There have been cases of Imams and religious teachers using boys and girls sexually. These veils simply veil the truth. It is time to break the silence about these taboo subjects.

Unfair to men

Veils cast all men as animalistic creatures with no control over their carnal natures, who are programmed to fall uninvited upon bosoms and lips, and have their way with any passing female (who, therefore, must wrap up in sheets and masks). Perhaps men should wear blindfolds? I see Muslim men everywhere in Britain, surrounded by non-veiled women. Most work, walk, shop, eat and drink and are not wild beasts full of lust. Decent and egalitarian Muslim men should be out protesting against this unfair characterisation.

---

38 'The Untold Story of How a Culture of Shame Perpetuates Abuse', *The Guardian*, 30 August 2014.

Sisterhood

Women who make the decision to veil are colluding with gender repression across the Muslim world. This choice cannot be separated from compulsion. It cannot be freestanding and severed from the savage imposition of the garment in many Arab lands, Pakistan, parts of Africa and, increasingly, western nations. We know Muslim women are forced into niqabs and chadors in Iran, Saudi Arabia, Afghanistan, parts of Nigeria and elsewhere, and that they are flogged if they don't, or worse. My question to those who freely choose to wear these coverings is this: What kind of sisterhood is this? When you know all this about enforced coverings, how do you not throw yours off in solidarity? In this country, parents forcing their girls to cover up use those who do so voluntarily as an example. Young girls tell me they are told: 'Look at them. They are real Muslims. You are full of sin if you don't follow them.' Reactionaries have persuaded outsiders that none of the females are coerced. Some do so of their own volition, others do not. They are either made to by adults or by their more 'obedient' mates. Independent

Muslim women who care about equality should take a stand and refuse to cover themselves. They should learn from those activists who refuse to wear clothes made by slave labour. Activism is about connections – the near and far – and political empathy.

Choices can be deceptive

The case of Shabina Begum was salutary. In 2002, the schoolgirl took her secondary school to court because it would not let her 'progress' from the hijab to the jilbab. She did not attend classes for two years and eventually won the case. For many of us modernist Muslims, this was a body blow. Her brother, a member of a defiantly anti-western Muslim group was, apparently, behind this decision. Her parents were dead. On appeal, her claim was rejected. The judge took the view that her full cover would put undue pressure on other Muslim pupils who were happy to wear the school uniform and that would disturb the delicate ecology of school life. Shabana Begum was clearly doing what her brother told her to, because he was her guardian. If girls are trained to make this choice, it is not a choice. In any case, this is not just a consumer choice, but one that is loaded with meanings and implications. I have spoken to several lots of sisters, all of whom cover up in some way. Not one felt able to dress freely. All said they could not go against family and community wishes.

There is such a thing as society

Segregation damages societies. Self-segregation does so too. Girls' schools in Britain are great for education, but often really damage self-esteem and wellbeing. So it is with veiled women, only more so. That must have consequences for integration, ambition and prospects. They inhabit a restricted space, real or imagined. That is not good for them or society. Veils send non-verbal messages: wearers have to stay within the fold and limit the range and depth of relationships with outsiders. Yes, some do in fact have good friends who are not from their tight circles, but those friendships are constrained. Can a Hindu or atheist girl stay the night with a veiled Muslim friend? What about vice versa?

Body image

Like other women around the world, veiled women can suffer from bad anxieties about their bodies, beauty and desirability. The onus is on them to obey and please men. The claim that they are released from those pressures is just another big beauty myth. While we talk openly and often about the negative impact of our perfectionist and sex-obsessed culture on other women and girls, hardly anyone dares to speak up about similar pressures on traditional Muslim females. It is time to discuss this issue honestly and publicly.

Brainwashing

In contemporary culture, women and girls are pushed into following the dictates of fashion – but they are not threatened or punished if they refuse to comply. Muslim females are programmed to obey and don't feel they can reject head or body coverings because that would make them pariahs in some communities. Research is needed into how the veil is spread and by whom, and, most importantly, the deep influences and pressures on females.

Health

Getting no sunlight leads to vitamin D deficiency. An Australian study carried out in 2009 confirmed this.[39] There is a resurgence in rickets and other bone diseases in Muslim communities. (They do, however, avoid the perils of skin cancer, caused by too much exposure to sunlight.) Far more serious is the domestic violence that can be concealed under niqabs and burkhas. Not all women in burkhas are the walking wounded, but some are, and the tragedy is that it is impossible to pick up the signs. The usual network of concerned people – neighbours, colleagues, pupils, teachers, police or social workers – would need to be approached by the traumatised women and girls, otherwise the problem would remain hidden.

Compulsion

We simply do not know how many women are compelled and how many choose to veil. We cannot assume

---

39 See www.islam-watch.org.

they are all choosing the garments. The problem is we can never know for certain. We do, however, know children are being made to cover up. Proselytisers are increasingly autocratic on this matter. The state needs to protect mothers and children from them. If it can't intervene directly, dress codes are the fairest way of dealing with the trend.

Obstacles to performance

Veils hamper proper professional functioning. You cannot teach, give evidence, drive, treat patients, deal with public service workers or be on the staff if you do not show your face. I would go further and say long cloaks too are a hindrance. Muslim women were just starting to join the workforce in greater numbers when veils began to spread. In 2005, Aishah Azmi decided to put on a niqab while working as a teaching assistant after, it is said, she was commanded to do so by a religious leader. She was sacked because she could not do her job properly. She took her case to tribunal, which dismissed her complaint. How sad is that? In that same year, Shabnam Mughal, a legal advisor, was asked by a judge to show her face and all hell broke loose. Eventually, the judiciary backed down. How do these women think they will get ahead? Interviewed by the journalist Andrew Anthony, Rahmanara Chowdhury, a teacher of interpersonal and communications skills in Loughborough, defended her burkha by saying she felt more empowered being just a voice. Well, soon some woman-hating Imam will pronounce that the voice or scent of a woman are too seductive to be allowed in public spaces.

Security and safety

Alan Johnson, who was in the Labour Education Secretary in 2007, gave schools the right to forbid veils on these grounds and also because he felt such segregation affected communal teaching. He was right, but because of noisy opposition this vital power fell into disuse. In recent years, Islamicist plots have got bolder. Niqabs could become the perfect disguise for those who want to create mayhem. Airports and borders have to find ways to deal with this possibility and yet not offend veiled women. This is unfair.

Commonalities matter more than differences

The banning of the headscarf in France was, in fact, supported by many Muslims. The state was too arrogant and confrontational but the policy was right. A secular public space gives all citizens civil rights and fundamental equalities and Muslim girls have not abandoned schools in droves as a result of the ban. I learnt another useful lesson on why it is important to disallow veils in a school in Delhi, where more than half the pupils were Muslims from traditional families. There was no hijab on the head of any of the girls. The headmistress told me this:

> Our job is to educate and create commonalities between the children, not to stress the differences. It is to create a real spirit of equality, similarity and togetherness. Tolerance of difference is a weak concept. Yes we are all individuals, and from various backgrounds, but we are,

in the end, all human. No parent has ever come in to ask
that their daughter should wear a hijab. Actually one did,
they had moved back from Blackburn. You are spreading these habits to us.

She said this laughingly, but she is right. America, a
deeply Christian nation, does not allow religion to
be manifested in schools either. We need educators
to be similarly clear and confident on what school is for.

Autonomy and individuality

This is a society that prizes autonomy and gender parity. The burkha offends both these principles. The meek
acceptance of the burkha by British feminists is baffling.
They must be repelled by the garment and its meanings. I know many of them do feel uncomfortable and
then bad about feeling uncomfortable. This is absurd
relativism. What are they afraid of? Afghani and Iranian women fight daily against the shroud and there is
nothing 'colonial' about raising ethical objections to
this obvious symbol of oppression. To the accusation

that questioning this sexist garb reinforces patriarchy, because it infringes a woman's right to decide how much or little to wear, I say prove to me that all the females have indeed chosen the veil. They can't. Therefore they cannot, in all honesty, make the claims they do.

Not a distraction, but a fundamental issue

Those of us who argue against the veil are told it's a red herring, a fuss about nothing – just dress, just clothes, that we should concentrate on the many bigger problems remain unsolved. This is sophistry and they know it. The feminists of Egypt and Iran back in the early part of the twentieth century were told the same. It didn't stop them. We should turn the argument around and ask: why do Muslims focus on female clothes when they have so many other big challenges? Poverty, unemployment, corruption, human rights violation do not get the attention they demand, but veils do. And so we who cannot accept them are bound to attend to the coverings too.

Distorted values

While non-Muslims fall over themselves to 'under-stand' and defend veils, the favour is not reciprocated. I do not hear conservative Muslims defending the rights of Muslim and non-Muslim women not to cover up. What if two teenage girls in the same family made their own choices – one to wear a hijab and the other to show her hair? Does anybody really think the second girl would not face anger and pressure? One Muslim writer asked in 2013: 'How safe and included do veiled Muslim women feel?' She did not ask the same question for non-veiled women who venture into Wahabi Islam enclaves. So I ask it here: 'Is a girl in a short skirt safe? Does she feel respected in Muslim areas of, say, Bradford?'

Identity, dissent and rebellions

I talk often to young veiled women to understand why they choose to cover up hair, bodies or faces. I realise for some it is a way of asserting cultural and religious distinctiveness, and for others, a way of irritating power and being rebellious. They do not want to be ground down to a uniform, western identity. That is indeed their right. I do admire their sense of themselves as part of a group. However, compromise is part of the social contract and it is not acceptable for this one part of society to refuse to give at all. Also, they must remember that the most extremist elements in our country also espouse the veil – only a minority, true, but they impact on the debate and choice.

Cohesion

A nation cannot, and should not, support all demands in the name of cultural preferences or religious obligations. In several schools already, Muslim parents are refusing to let their girls swim, act, play music, go on trips or take part in PE – interference that should not be tolerated. Veils are only one part of a bigger movement away from modernity and progressive values. It is insulting and also seems to cast aspersions on women who are not covered up. The message is: those who veil have morals, you are immoral. To white women the message is even more unkind: because you don't veil, you are presumed to have no morals or boundaries. The veil also indicates that females accept their various, burdensome roles: they are carriers of collective virtue; guarantors of sexual 'purity'; guards who stop western values crossing the threshold; subservient marriage partners, daughters, sisters, nieces, sisters-in-law, aunts, grans and so on. Subservient, that is, to all males in the family. Those women who do enter politics or get to the top of professions by donning a scarf, cloak or face cover again announce their inferiority or jeopardy to males and, of course, superiority to the females whose faces, arms, legs, hair, necks and cleavages are not kept under wraps.

Racism

Over the last decade, the rise of extreme right parties across Europe is leading to racism directed at all people of colour and migrants, and, most of all, those who 'look Muslim'. I have witnessed hijabis and niqabis verbally insulted, spat at and sometimes pushed by white men and women. I have also seen the looks of anger and hatred they get. These women must be protected. The police and courts have not taken this issue seriously and they should. However, racism is too often used to stop debates and policies on veiling. We should be able to confront the evil of racism without giving in to obscurantist practices.

European law

In July 2014, the European Court of Human Rights in Strasbourg upheld the French law banning niqabs in public spaces. In 2008, that same court backed the French ban on headscarves in schools. The latest ruling did not mention any faith but concluded that the court was able to 'understand the view that individuals might not wish to see, in places open to all, practices and attitudes which would fundamentally call into question the possibility of open, interpersonal relationships, which, by virtue of an established consensus, formed an indispensable part of community life within the society in question'. This is a remarkably sensitive and bold declaration. It is one Britain's governing classes should take seriously.

Our society is a complex tapestry of various beliefs, practices, inclinations, lifestyles, differences and prejudices. It is intricate and relatively strong – but not that strong. If exclusion on grounds of race, gender, age and religion is wrong, then so too is self-exclusion.

I rest my case.

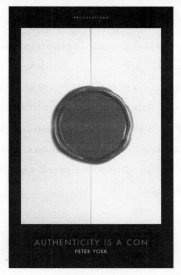